Motivation to My Generation

Leaving a Legacy

Sadiyyah Latimer

authorHOUSE®

AuthorHouse™
1663 Liberty Drive
Bloomington, IN 47403
www.authorhouse.com
Phone: 1-800-839-8640

First published by AuthorHouse   10/22/2009

ISBN: 978-1-4490-3904-2 (e)
ISBN: 978-1-4490-3747-5 (sc)

Library of Congress Control Number: 2009910837

Printed in the United States of America
Bloomington, Indiana

This book is printed on acid-free paper.

My motivation to my generation is an inspirational & motivational collection of phrases and quotes on the value of speaking and planting the seeds of life to see results . It is guaranteed to provide wisdom, knowledge and direction to everyone .This book will motivate you to make dreams a reality and be what you see positively. You have invested in your next chapter. Keep on looking up there is more ahead.

Complemented by beautiful photographs of aspiring children, successful adults, political and religious leaders, celebrities, models and actors. These thoughts and sayings are sure to motivate anyone to accomplish their dream.

A Good listeners answer becomes the solution to a unresolved problem.

Understanding where people
are in life is more beneficial
then knowing the reason.

God loves us inside out.
People love us outside in.

We fail by trying and
achieve by doing.

It's not how much you make but how much you invest in the right things

Singleness is a lifestyle not
defined by loneliness.

Knowledge applied equals power.
Power is knowing the extent of your
ignorance for favorable results.

Think like a warrior who's a leader,
and lead like a warrior who thinks.

I serve my generation so that my
assignment won't be incomplete.

Considerate people are confident
but never coincident.

One step forward is better than no mobility at all. Future Forward Focus

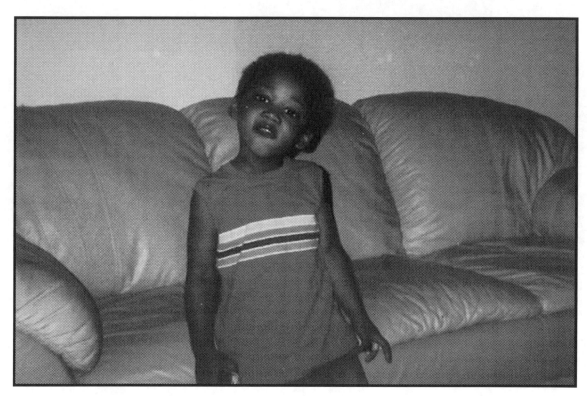

Being friendly attracts
people of understanding.

Progress is an outward
statement of growth.

The weapon of silence is good
for a fight that doesn't take
words of wisdom to win.

God is love. Love is real.

What matters in the end is
not where you have been but
what you have learned.

The biggest enemy is the
inner you. Take ownership
& responsibility of your own
mistakes only. Become educated

The Grave use to be one of the richest places of people dying with their dreams left in them until I was born.

The greatest victory is the
one over your inner sin. Look
from God's perspective

Look people in the face and
know them for who they are
not for what they offer.

If you do not obtain everything
you pray for, pray for everything
in Christ's will for you.

Silence is only important
when wisdom is her coach.

A legacy in generations are
not made by complainers.

When I grow up I don't
want to be a wanna be.

Some people fail at focus and
others just need more faith.

Real Kings stand for something
only thugs settle for destruction.

A person that steals vision
from others cannot see the
character they lack.

Family is vital so pay attention
to their sign language.

Maturity is the key to mental growth, which equals results. Listen to learn and not to judge

Temporary items aren't worth
having all now to loose later.
Stability is the key I need

The impossible is tangible once
you believe you can grab it.

You believe what you say. You say what you believe and you have what you work hard for

Why serve Satan who rebelled then fell selling your soul when mankind destiny wasn't supposed to be hell.

Jail is not a place but a
state of mind. Be free

Only feed the seed in you,
you need to succeed.

Time wasted means you
never owned it.

A moment used wisely is worth
more than being rich for a lifetime.

Reality = A dream with
action to back it.

Over comers say I can do,
under achievers say I can't.

Why settle when I can set standards. I'm the passenger while My Father drives.

Goals are for movers and shakers
while daydreamers procrastinate

There are no opportunity's
available for failure.

Let your life teach while
your words reach

I Prevail

When you yield to negativity, you
have advance hells assignment

Refuse to be a statistic and
dare to be different.

Stand when you want to fall,
laugh when you want to cry,
love when you want to hate and
live when you want to die.

Self respect is more important
than celebrity status.

Shallow people produce
fruitless points.

Booking info

For booking information
Email slatimer08@yahoo.com
Phone: 1 (302) 218-1300
website: www.sadiyyahlatimer.com

Cover Design
Cover by: Anthony Jermaine
Innerkube Design Lab
www.innerkube.net

Printed in the United States
by Baker & Taylor Publisher Services